DARREN FIELD
PRESENTS

Vault of the Macabre

For;

Mum, Dad, James, Jane, Adam, Clive, Cassandra,
Ted, Larry, Samantha, Heather and Russell. ~ **Thank you!**

All that we see or seem -
is but a dream within a dream.

~Edgar Allan Poe

contents

CONTENTS

THE MISGUIDED DIVINATION OF VICTORIA

On Halloween night
In the pale moon light
There once was a man
Who had quite a fright

He looked in the mirror
And turned out the light
And proceeded to call
With all of his might

Call on a spirit
A ghost in the ether
A ghost who was known
As a furious soul eater

The legend it says
That on Halloween night
When the veil between worlds
Can be lifted from sight

That you call on a ghost
And you beckon it near
And turn out the lights
Then said ghost will appear

This ghost in particular
Was a beautiful sight
With flowing red hair
And skin pale and white

She died long ago
At the hands of her lover
And now walks the Earth
As reaper of others

The man in question
Thought the legend so daft
That when he called out her name
He started to laugh

But his laughter soon ceased
As the darkness ensued
And out from the shadows
Victoria pursued

With ashen skin
And eyes black as coal
Victoria had come
To claim this man's soul

He let out a scream
But nothing was heard
No pleading or begging
Not even a word

Victoria had taken
Another mans soul
And left in it's place
A dark rotting hole

Her fury and pain
Once more had been sated
For now, at least
Til' next young man bated

And dared to call
The name of Victoria
And then once more dies
In her gothic euphoria

So Halloween legends
Do not take for granted
That a ghost will not come
And kill the faint hearted

All Hallow's eve
A night filled with magic
Can if you're not careful
End bloody and tragic…

Happy Halloween.

Narcoleptic Nell

Nell was a woman so fair of face
Whenever she moved she did it with grace

As she'd enter a room she'd light up the place
Then all of a sudden she'd fall on her face

THE MACABRE MADNESS OF MORTULIA MOROSE

Mortulia Morose had a strange disposition
She loved all things gruesome, gothic and forbidden
Her life at times would seem rather dull
She lived alone with just a cat and a skull

The skull once belonged to her dead husband Bart
Whom she killed with an axe, then hacked up the parts
She loved her husband with all of her heart
But would love him more dead, unfortunately for Bart

So forever alone she sits in her tomb
Just her and the cat, the skull and her doom
For Mortulia you see, is now quite mad
The murder took away any sanity she had

PRESTON

Preston Parker was a curious fellow

His face was blue and his eyes were yellow

His arms swayed in front

And his legs dragged behind

And he walked with a limp

And in circles at times

His jawbone was loose
And his spine broke in two

His elbows exposed
And no toes in his shoes

But fear not for Preston
He was in no pain

Instead he's a zombie
In search of some brains

MYRTLE BERTLE AND THE SUSPICIOUS DISSAPPEARANCE OF THE NEIGHBOUR BABIES

Myrtle Bertle was a lovely lady
The problem was, that she liked to eat babies

She'd boil them up in a rather large pot
Or roast in the oven with mushrooms and shallots

The neighbours never once suspected or knew
That Myrtle liked to cook babies in stew

THE BALLAD OF STINGY JACK

Stingy Jack
Stingy Jack
Teeth of Yellow
Heart of Black

Couldn't go to heaven
Couldn't go to hell
Even the devil
Didn't want you as well

He gave you a rock
As black as your heart
A chalky burning ember
To see in the dark

Walking through the woods
You hear a faint sound
You go to cry out
But there's no one around

Whatever you do
Don't let the light
In your fat orange pumpkin
Stop burning bright

For if it goes out
Jack will appear
He'll come from behind
With a smile ear to ear

He'll rip out your eyes
And bite off your tongue
He'll try to steal your soul
And he'll leave you with none

Jack walks the earth
Alone in the dark
With only an ember
to light his path

So if you meet jack
Run for your life
Cos he'll soon draw blood
And he wont need a knife

He'll rip out your throat
And bash in your brains
He'll pull out your heart
And he'll eat the remains

JAMES THE PUMPKIN HEADED BOY

James was born with a pumpkin for a head

So come Halloween, he'd carve children instead.

Tarquin Pope and His Numerous Unsuccessful Suicide Attempts

Tarquin Pope just Couldn't die
Even though he'd try and he'd try
He never really knew
Or understood why

He'd drown himself
Or cut off his face
But then soon after
One grew back in it's Place

He'd jump under a train
Or drink Sulfuric acid
Or hang from a noose
Til' his body became flaccid

But then soon after
He popped back to life
So he'd try once again
Maybe this time with a knife

So there he would sit
planning new ways to try
Because all Taquin wanted
Was to finally die

Frank the Manic Depressive Mummy

There was once a mummy
Buried deep in his tomb
Who suffered from such
An unbearable gloom

The Mummy named Frank
Had been there for years
But his sanity had ceased
And over come with fears

With thoughts so morose
Bouncing round in his head
After all these years
Frank was rather depressed.

Well wouldn't you be too,
After all, he is dead!

Nathaniel

Nathaniel Jones was just like you or I
Everyone said he was a really sweet guy

But secretly Nathaniel heard voices in his head
Voices that told him certain people should be dead.

Rumour has it Nathaniel was a serial killer
He'd strangle your neck or pull out your liver

He's a really nice guy, just a shame he's a killer.

Goodnight

Do you ever hear those voices in the dark?
Voices that threaten to rip you apart?
Chances are it's nothing at all
Just your imagination playing tricks quite cruel

When you slip into bed
Snuggle deep beneath the covers
Telling yourself you're alone
There's no others…

Or maybe there's someone in the shadows that dwell
At the end of your bed
In the darkness…
Sleep well.

PETER THE PARANOID PENGUIN

Peter was a penguin at the local city zoo.

He was convinced that there was an impending zombie apocalypse orchestrated by the giraffe's in the next enclosure, intent on world domination...

Peter was wrong.

THE IMAGINARY WORLD OF DORIAN JAMES

Dorian James was a strange little boy.
His days it seemed were filled with very little joy.

Dorian you see, had no friends
Instead he would sit for hours on end

He'd rather fight dragons and zombies instead
These stores of course, were all in his head

Alone in his room
He would play pretend

Make up far away worlds
To mend and defend

Slay demons and monsters and save the damsel
Or thwart villainous schemes by some fella named Hansel

However alone Dorian may seem
By society standards a freak he's deemed

But in Dorian's head he has all the friends he needs
A monkey called Roy and a goblin called Reed

Vincent the Remorseful Voodoo Doll

Vincent felt really bad about the pain he had caused.

THE LUNA LUNACY OF LAWRENCE LONGHORN

Lawrence Longhorn was the last of a long line
In a family who believed they could transform into canine.

The family suffered from the disease of lycanthropy
A curse inflicted at the hands of a gypsy

For three nights a month under the fullest moon
Lawrence would transform and escape his tomb

He'd go on a rampage through the village near by
Causing murder and mayhem and other such crimes

Until one fateful evening Lawrence was caught
They shackled and bound him and took him to court

The judge had ruled Lawrence clearly insane
So he sent him to Midhirst, a hospital for the brain

Once inside the padded asylum walls
The doctors soon realized Lawrence not a werewolf at all

But rather a lunatic who's murderous doom
Was brought on by the various phases of the moon

So three nights a month when the moon shone bright
Lawrence was driven to kill in the moonlight.

Every so often when the first night arrives
You can still hear poor Lawrence when his curse does arise

A blood curdling howl as the phases shift
And Lawrence's bones and skin start to twist

But no fur or fangs or four legged fiend in his cell to be found
Just little Lawrence laying naked on the ground

Howling at the moon through barred window in his room
Lawrence was quite human, and imprisoned in his tomb

THE WORLD ACCORDING TO JANE

Jane hated everyone
She wanted them all dead
So one day she got a knife
And cut off peoples heads

At first she started slowly
With the people who upset her
Like the checkout girl who was too slow
Or the postman who lost her letter

But eventually Jane decided
That the world deserved to die
So she started hacking indiscriminately
At anyone who passed her by

And now she is much happier
With no people in her life
For she's now known as that crazy witch
Who'll cut you with a knife.

THE UNFORTUNATE TALE OF ICHABOD BLACK

Ichabod Black was not like other boys
He had no interest in sports, girls or toys
Instead he would sit alone in his room
And talk to himself and stare at the moon

But little Ichabod had a secret to keep
For it was not himself, but a friend he would speak
A boy named Tiberius, he came from the moon
He would sit and play in Ichabod's room

Ichabod's parents were worried it's true
For Ichabod's friend was invisible too
They thought their son crazy, a mental of sorts
Of course they still loved him, regardless of thoughts

But Poor little Ichabod was not for this world
As it turns out Tiberius was not there at all
But rather the symptom of a clot in Ich's brain
He died in an instant, and he felt no pain.

The Cautionary Tale of Maudlin Monroe

Maudlin Monroe wished he was dead.
A lunatic broke in and bashed in his head.

THE DIRGE OF THE JUMP ROPE GIRLS

Three little girls that lived down the road
Play jump rope together in their crisp white clothes

Two of the girls got bored with the game
They informed the third, Samantha her name

They wanted to know, could little girls fly
They walked Sam to the tree and proceeded to tie

They noosed the jump rope around the tall tree
And harked for Samantha to come and look see

She perched on a tire and poked her head through
As the other two girls watched her swing in the noose

The tire rolled from under her feet
And Samantha just wriggled and wobbled and freaked

The two little girls stood either side
Of the swinging corpse and looked on with pride

As now they know little girls can't fly.

DaVE †HE DEMEN†ED HERMI†

Dave was a man who liked the dark
He lived all alone in a house by the park

He wore moth eaten clothes and stared an eerie stare
He had conversations with people that weren't there.

With a maniacal laugh and spiders in his hair,
Not a bit of normality about him was there.

THE CURIOUS CONFINEMENT OF CONSTANCE ODDBALL

Constance Oddball never left her house
She lived with two sons, Colin and Klaus

Colin would bark, Klaus talk to trees
Constance would stare and complain with ease

But Constance it seems was a troubled mother
For she feared for the lives of Klaus and his brother

The boys were born different it's true
The Brothers they say were completely blue

A medical marvel with no explanation
But as you can see causes much complication

For Constance life was an endless routine
Of cooking and cleaning and seeming quite mean

The neighbour kids laughed and called her a witch
The parents made fun and called her a bitch

But Constance was sure if she let the world in
That her Boys would be mocked and taunted and things

So Constance lives a life of seclusion
To protect her blue boys from the worlds intrusion

THE SUDDEN AND INEVITABLE INSANITY OF GEORGE

George was normal
Then went insane
It was sadly unavoidable
As his mum was the same

But George however
Took insanity quite well
He was always quite a lonely lad
Never a friend or companion he had

But now George it seems is never alone
As he sits in his cell, all padded and chrome
For George now has what he always did seek
Someone to chat and laugh with and speak

The voices he hears, silent to others
In there somewhere is the voice of his mother's
The lonely boy not a friend in the world
Sits in his room, oh the stories he tells

Finally George it seems can be free
And it's all because of his sudden insanity

THE UNFORTUNATE DEATH OF GLIMMER VON— VANDAVORT

There once was a witch called Glimmer
She liked to eat children for dinner
Roasted with onions
Or cooked in a soup

Or baked in a pudding
With sage and vermouth
But one dull grey evening
Glimmer did fright

She choked on a child
The elbow of Mike
She writhed and she wiggled
All covered in sauce

The elbow still stuck
Not moving of course
She gasped and she screamed
Then fell to the bed

Then all of a sudden
The old witch was dead

THE DANCE OF PUMPKIN PATCH BILL

In the middle of a field where the Pumpkins grow
A top a hay bale stands a scarecrow
His clothes are moth eaten
His head is askew

His stuffing is loose
And his neck tie is blue
But every so often
If you look close enough

You'll see the scarecrow
Does seem to adjust
In the light of the moon
When it shines so bright

The Scarecrow named Billy
Jumps down from his height
He wonders the patch
Where the pumpkins grow

And dances around
In the cool moon glow
And if you should see
Scarecrow Bill dancing there

Whatever you do
Don't stop and stare
Just go on your way
And forget the crazed sight

Or the scarecrow named Bill
Will come kill you that night

TRICK OR TREAt

Trick or treat the children yelled
Dressed as witches and devils from hell

Give us some candy
They pleaded with glee

But no one did answer
And the lights went swiftly

The children stood 'neath the buzzing porch light
As the house in front sat dark in the night

But trick or treat the children yelled
And still not a whisper or presence was felt

Again calls unanswered
The house stayed the same

So the children decided
To play a new game

They made their way
To the back of the house

And slipped through the back door
Quiet as a mouse

Inside the house
They found the old lady

Watching TV
And drinking a Baileys

They got out some rope
And tied to the chair

The little old lady
With greyest of hair

They cut off her fingers
Replaced them with Kit Kats

And stuffed her ears full
With skittles and tic-tacs

They cut out her tongue
And fed it to the cat

Then lopped off her head
And sat on the mat

They removed the eyes
And hollowed the brain

Then carved out a smile
That looked quite insane

They inserted a candle
And then struck a match

Now the little old lady
Is not coming back

BORIS THE GRAVE ROBBER

Boris was a grave robber
He was the best around,

He pilfered your valuables
From under the ground,

But one fateful night
In the tomb of Sally Stave,

Boris hit his head
And fell in Sally's grave,

When morning did come
Boris did not arise,

Instead grave diggers came
And buried Boris alive

THE FOOLISH PURSUIT OF ETERNAL YOUTH

Low and behold
The three sisters grim
With beady black eyes
And pale green skin

Surrounded a pot
All bubbling with heat
They threw in some eye balls
And a few severed feet

They conjured some words
An ancient lost language
Then tossed in the pot
An old rotting sandwich

They each shook their head
And spat in the pot
Then breathed through their noses
And threw in some snot

Faster

Feaster

Mother

Brother

Catcher

Killer

Eater

Smother

When the last word was spoke
The witches stood back
And a puff of red smoke
Engulfed their whole shack

The witches were turned
From pasty pale hags
To gorgeous fair maidens
All perky and glad

But the spell would not last
As the witches would see
For their magic's were older
Than the sisters three

Instead they grew younger
Back through the days
Younger and younger
Till nothing remained

All that was left
As their hopes were dashed
Was a bubbling pot
And three piles of ash

Be careful what you wish
One might say
Is the moral of the story
And the theme of the day

POPPY

Poppy Marshall wanted nothing more
Than to be a cheerleader and watch her team score

To ensure success at her cheerleader tryouts
She followed Anne home and poked both her eyes out

To the back of the school she stalked Kelly-Sue
Put a bag on her head until she turned blue

She saw Sarah Jane at the swimming pool that night
Then doused her with petrol and set her Alight

Then finally she came to little Marie
She smothered with honey and set loose some bees

And the next day at school Poppy was pleased
For her cheerleader try out went with greatest of ease

With no competition she was sure of a place
But the cheerleader captain just laughed in her face

She called Poppy fat and an utter disgrace
To which Poppy threw some acid in her face

As you can probably tell poppy was quite insane
And you probably assume that her parents to blame

But the fact of the matter is Poppy was born
With a predisposition to maim and to scorn

Poppy escaped and is still on the loose
With maybe a knife and perhaps a loose noose

So if you happen to notice the new girl in town
Whatever you do don't make her frown

For chances are with the world so small
That the girl in question is Poppy Marshall

BETTY'S APPLE PIE

Betty Rose Nivens was famous no lie
For baking the world's best apple pie
She baked them with love and care and attention
But the secret ingredient she never did mention

People would come from miles around
To sample the pie the talk of the town
But if only they knew that baked in the pie
Was the flesh of some children that Betty made die

She'd lure them in with candy and treats
Then once inside she'd hang by their feet
She placed in a cage the children she caught
Then fattened them up with chocolate and pork

She then chopped the children up so fine
Then mixed in the apples and raisins and wine
Preheated the oven to three sixty degrees
Then placed in the pie with the greatest of ease

The smell of the pie would glide through the town
She'd place on the window to let it cool down
And the town never knew nor suspected a thing
That the Pie they were eating made with children missing

MAURICE THE MOROSE CLOWN

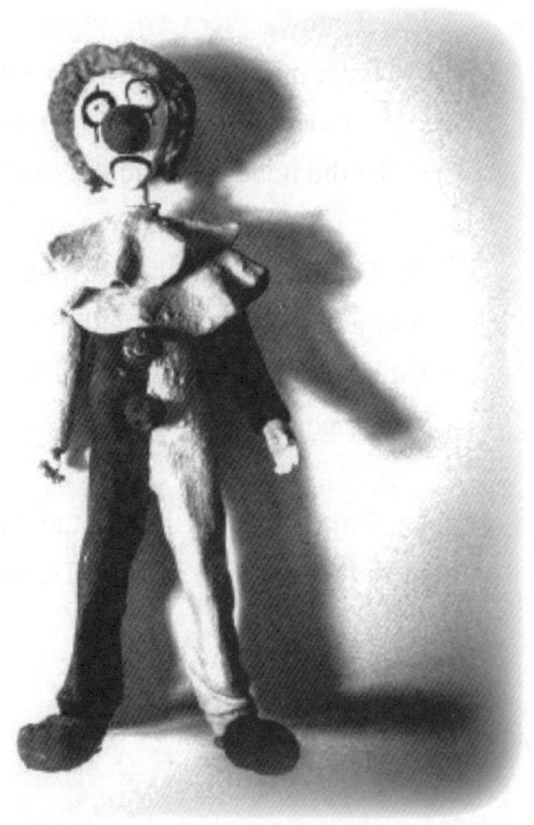

Maurice was a Morose Clown
He didn't get much work.

WHY CHILDREN SHOULD LISTEN TO MOTHER

Little Timmy Tyler went swimming in the sea
Having minutes before just eaten his tea
His mother did warn of the perils await
If he did not digest and the full hour wait

But Timmy ignored the warnings from mum
And jumped in the sea with food in his tum
He swam out a little then suddenly stopped
And then Timmy's belly did suddenly pop

Timmy exploded as mother had said
His dinner was floating and Timmy was dead

THE PERILS OF THE ZOO

David's life was a sad one its true
He's parents died visiting at the state Zoo
His mother fell in the lions pit first
Then his father dived in
And was lions desert

So David grew up
Afraid of the zoo
But to be quite fair
Wouldn't you have been too?

Betty's Halloween Candy

Betty Rose Nivens did Love Halloween
She loved giving candy and hearing kids scream

She carved out her pumpkins
With love and with care

And hung ghosts and goblins
Up over the stair

When her door bell would ring
And the kids trick or treat

Mountains of candy
She gave them to eat

But Betty Rose Nivens
Was not what she seemed

As the candy she gave them
Was ever so mean

The chocolate bars stuffed
With sharp razor blades

And the pumpkin shaped cookies
With arsenic she laced

In the orange striped lollies
Rat poison she dropped

And the soft cantered chews
Some boils she popped

For Betty you see
Did love Halloween

But the children it brought
She'd rather not see

So every year On October 31st
Betty Rose Nivens her cupboards would burst

With poisons and potions
And other foul treats

To feed to the children
Buried inside their sweets

All this she did was incredibly mean
All so Ms. Nivens could enjoy Halloween

THE HEARTBREAK OF THE SKELETON BOY

Bartholomew Tucker was born with no skin
No muscles or hair and no organs within

Instead he was born a skeleton boy
A fact to his parents that brought little joy

They put up dear Bart for adoption at once
But who in right mind would give poor Bart a glance

One stormy night after 12 years unwanted
Bart packed up his teddy and quickly departed

He travelled the world Just Bart and his teddy
And on the way round good friends not made any

To this very day Bart still is alone
Just he and his teddy his stuffing all shown

If ever you see skeleton Bart in the distance
Do him a favour just note his existence

Give him a smile and a wave and a hug
You'll make poor Bart's day and he'll finally feel love

DR. ED

There once was a dentist called Ed
He was in fact quite demented
He drilled for his pleasure
Much to his delight

He caused his patients
Much pain and such fright
Because Ed you see
Is utterly demented

His procedure you see
Really should be prevented
So patients beware
If your dentist is Ed

You really shouldn't let
Ed loose on your head
For the last one that did
Is currently dead

THE PLIGHT OF GUSTAV GORE

Gustav Gore, people would say
Did never seem to go out in the day

Which led them to speculate that he must be ill
But Gustav's affliction was graver still

You see, Gustav was not like you or like I
He could turn into Smoke and bats and could fly

He shied away from daylight and fire
Because you see, Gustav was a vampire

THE YOUNG LOVERS

Bonnie and Nathan were prom king and queen
They drove lovers cove where they couldn't be seen

Whilst the pair got quite amorous
They did suddenly pause

As Nathan it seems got a nature call
He stepped to the Bushes

Disappeared in the Dark
Leaving dear Bonnie alone in car parked

First she heard tapping, and then faint foot steps
She turned on the radio and the news caster said

ATTENTION ATTENTION!! breaking news
A nutter escaped from estate in the mews

Last he was seen on highway 19
report to police if again he is seen

Bonnie flipped on the cars high beam lights
And the sign that she saw gave Bonnie a fright

The car was parked adjacent to sign
Highlighting the path to Highway One Nine

She called out to Nathan but he'd not reply
For Nathan was dead in a ditch quite near by

Bonnie then heard the tapping again
This time quite louder and still it remained

Scared for her life Bonnie started the car
She drove herself home as it wasn't that far

An hour had passed since Bonnie was home
All tucked up in bed waiting Nathan to phone

A good night's sleep Bonnie was not to get
She tossed and she turned all full of regret

But comforted by her puppy dog Titch
As Bonnie would stir her toes he would lick

And early next morning Bonnie did rise

And painted on the wall to Bonnie's surprise

Was a sign that read it is said to be true

Yes my dear Bonnie, humans can lick too

The story goes the message was written

In the blood of Nathan with whom she was smitten

So it would seem the previous night

Much to Bonnie's total fright

That just outside, in the back of the car

Was escaped lunatic Samuel K Bar